digging in the dirt

A Kid's Guide to How Fruit Grows

Patricia Ayers

The Rosen Publishing Group's
PowerKids Press™
New York

Published in 2000 by The Rosen Publishing Group, Inc.
29 East 21st Street, New York, NY 10010

First Edition

Book Design: Maria Melendez

Photo Credits: Cover and title page, pp. 1, 4, 7, 8, 9, 10, 13, 18, 21 © Super Stock; pp. 7, 14, 17 © Tony Stone Images; p. 7 © International Stock

Photo Illustrations: pp. 11, 12, 15, 16, 19, 20, 22 © Andy Comins

A special thanks to Jim Bailey from Centennial Farms at the Orange County Fairgrounds, 88 Fair Dr., Costa Mesa, CA 92626, for giving Andy Comins a hand in creating these magnificent pictures.

Ayers, Patricia.
        A kid's guide to how fruit grows / by Patricia Ayers.
            p.   cm. — (The Digging in the dirt series)
    Includes index.
    Summary: Explains the basics of growing different kinds of fruit and gives simple instructions for planting and growing strawberries.
    ISBN: 0-8239-5466-8 (lib. bdg.)
    1. Fruit-culture—Juvenile literature.   2. Fruit—Juvenile literature.
    [1. Fruit culture. 2. Strawberries.] I. Title.
    II. Series: Ayers, Patricia. Digging in the dirt series.

SB357.2.A94   1999
634—dc21   98-51631
                                                                                                          CIP
                                                                                                          AC

Manufactured in the United States of America

Contents

13,25

How Fruit Grows

When you eat a piece of fruit, you probably don't think about where it came from. Did you know that bananas grow on trees in upside-down bunches and that pineapples grow close to the ground on a stalk? Many fruits don't look alike or grow in the same way, but they all carry **seeds** and can be eaten, either by people or animals. The tough coconut that grows 100 feet up on a palm tree is a fruit. An olive is a fruit, too. Some fruit seeds are big, like the ones inside avocados and peaches. Others are tiny, like the little brown ones inside bananas. The coconut has the biggest seed in the world.

◁ *Fruits and their seeds come in many shapes and sizes.*

5

Fruit on the Move

Most fruit has come to America from other places. Fruit tastes so good that people have carried their seeds from place to place for thousands of years. Peaches and oranges were first grown in China and India. Apple seeds were brought to America from Europe. Bananas first came from Southeast Asia, but now grow mostly in Central America. Different fruits grow in different **climates**. Fruits like apples need a cold season when the trees can rest, or stop growing. Citrus fruits, like oranges and grapefruits, grow best in warm weather but can live through a frost. **Tropical** fruits like bananas can't stand the cold at all.

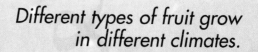

Different types of fruit grow in different climates. ▶

Peach Tree

Apple Tree

Orange Tree

Banana Tree

How Fruit Gets Sweet

No matter what climate they're in, all fruit plants need sunshine, water, and soil to grow. The plants grow roots that draw in water and **nutrients** from the soil. Veins in the plant stems or tree trunks carry the water and nutrients to the leaves. Leaves contain a substance called **chlorophyll** that makes them green. Chlorophyll absorbs energy from the sunlight. The energy helps to turn water, nutrients, and air into sugar that will feed the plant or tree and make the fruit sweet. This process is called **photosynthesis**. Thanks to photosynthesis, people and animals can eat sweet and healthy fruit.

◀ *Fruit gets sweeter as it grows and ripens.*

Growing Strawberries

Mr. Chan's class decided to grow strawberries. The bright red, sweet and juicy strawberry will grow almost anywhere. Mr. Chan's class knew that a strawberry bed can last for years, so they wanted to prepare it well. In spring, when the dirt was crumbly and warm, they measured a rectangle, four feet wide by eight feet long, on a sunny piece of ground. They dug about eight inches deep and removed any stones, weeds, and grass they found. Then they measured out four rows, each a foot apart from the next, where they would plant the strawberry plants.

Mr. Chan's class prepared the strawberry bed by digging up the dirt and turning it over. ▷

Sweet and Sour Dirt

Mr. Chan told the class that different fruits grow better in different soil depending on how acid or alkaline the soil is. Soil is called acid or "sour" when it has a lot of **sulfur**. Soil is called alkaline or "sweet" when it's rich in **lime**. The class learned that strawberries need dirt that is a little acid, or sour. The class used a soil test kit to see if their dirt was acid or alkaline. It turned out their dirt was just sour enough to grow strawberries, but that it needed more **nitrogen**.

Mr. Chan had **fertilizer** handy for this purpose. Fertilizer is a material, usually made from manure or **compost** that is full of nutrients like nitrogen. The class mixed in the fertilizer to help the berries grow big and fat.

◀ *You can change the soil from alkaline to acid by adding sulfur or lime to the dirt.*

Planting Strawberry Spiders

You can buy young fruit plants from most garden stores. Mr. Chan bought strawberry plants in bundles of 25. When the students picked up the plants, they thought they looked like spiders. The top, where the leaves sprouted, looked like the head of a spider. The head of the strawberry plant is also called the **crown**. The roots dangled down from the crown like legs. Mr. Chan told the class to put each plant in the ground so the roots would spread underground and the head would be barely covered with dirt. The students spaced the plants one foot apart from each other, filled in the dirt around the plants, and patted the dirt gently but firmly.

The root on this strawberry spider plant will soon crawl through the dirt. ▷

Growing a Fruit Family

All plants need water to grow. Mr. Chan's class watered each strawberry plant making sure the roots got enough to drink. In a few days the strawberry heads popped up out of the dirt. That meant they were planted just right. One student poked her finger in the soil every day to see if it was dry and needed water. One day, she noticed long stems from the plants running along the ground. These were **runners** the strawberry plants sent out to grow daughter plants. The runners grow roots and then start new plants. Only a few types of fruit plants grow runners.

◁ *It's important to check the soil regularly and water it when it's dry.*

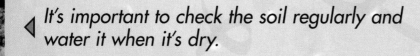

Strawberry Blossoms

The class watched the garden daily. They picked any of the weeds that grew, so they wouldn't get in the way of the strawberry plants. A month later, one of the boys in the class spotted the first white flowers. Plants grow flowers in order to **reproduce**. Inside of flowers, there is something called **pollen**. Pollen is a fine powder, usually yellow, that is the male part of the plant. It needs to mix with the female part of another plant to **fertilize** it. Mr. Chan's class learned that bees, birds, and the wind help move pollen to the female part of the plant. This is called **pollination**. Pollination leads to fertilization. Only fertilized flowers can make seeds.

First, the strawberry plants grow flowers. Later, they will grow fruit. ▷

Why Plants Grow Fruit

   Plants grow fruit in order to protect their seeds and to help them scatter around in different directions. The more places the seeds are scattered, the better chance they will have for survival. A coconut seed, for example, can float a great distance on water and then grow into a tree wherever it lands. Other fruits can be blown far away by the wind. The bumpy ride may damage the fruit, but not the seed. Fruit is also eaten by birds and other animals. When the seeds pass through them, the seeds will be planted in the earth where they can grow. Fruit helps seeds grow far and wide.

◁ *Coconut seeds are protected by a tough shell that can float on water.*

Harvest Time

Over time the white flower petals fell off the strawberry plants and left behind hard, greenish berries. These began to grow and ripen into big red strawberries. In another month, the class was able to **harvest** their first ripe berries. They had to search under the leaves of the plants to find all the strawberries. Mr. Chan told the class it was important to pick all the strawberries. Otherwise, the plants would stop growing them. Each student collected a full basket of strawberries to bring home. They also got to look forward to next year, when the fruit would start growing again!

Glossary

chlorophyll (KLOR-uh-fil) A substance that give green plants their color and allows them to make food.

climates (KLY-mits) The weather conditions of certain places.

compost (KOM-post) Decaying vegetables used as fertilizer.

crown (KROWN) The part of a plant between the root and the stem.

fertilize (FUR-tuh-lyz) To make a plant start to grow.

fertilizer (FUR-tuh-ly-zer) A nutrient-rich substance that helps crops grow.

harvest (HAR-vist) A season's gathered crops.

lime (LYM) A white substance used to improve soil.

nitrogen (NY-tro-jen) A colorless, ordorless element that is good for many plants.

nutrients (NEW-tree-ents) Anything that a living thing needs for energy, to grow, or to heal.

photosynthesis (fo-to-SIN-thuh-sis) The process by which green plants use sunlight to make their own food from carbon dioxide and water.

pollen (PAH-lin) A fine powder from the male part of the plant that fertilizes the female part of the plant.

pollination (pah-lih-NAY-shun) A carrying or moving of pollen to other flowers.

reproduce (ree-pruh-DOOS) To make more of something of the same kind. To have babies.

runners (RUN-ers) Long stems that run along the surface of the ground and send out roots and leaves.

seeds (SEEDZ) A part of the plant from which another plant can grow.

sulfur (SUL-fer) A chemical element that makes soil more acid, or sour.

tropical (TROH-pih-kuhl) From a hot and sunny area near the middle of the earth.

Index

Web Sites:

You can learn more about how fruit grows on the Internet. Check out these web sites:

24 http://www.urbanext.uiuc.edu/gpe/index.html
http://aggiie.horticulture.tamu.edukinder/funpage.html